Celebrate!

Italy

Robyn Hardyman

W
FRANKLIN WATTS
LONDON•SYDNEY

This edition first published in 2009
by Franklin Watts

Copyright © 2009
The Brown Reference Group Ltd

Franklin Watts
338 Euston Road
London NW1 3BH

Franklin Watts Australia
Level 17/207 Kent Street
Sydney, NSW 2000

A CIP catalogue record for this book is available
from the British Library.
Dewey no: 914.5

ISBN 978 0 7496 8426 6

Printed in China

Franklin Watts is a division of Hachette Children's Books,
an Hachette UK company.
www.hachette.co.uk

For The Brown Reference Group Ltd
Project Editor: Sarah Eason
Designer: Paul Myerscough
Picture Researcher: Maria Joannou
Indexer: Claire Throp
Design Manager: David Poole
Managing Editor: Miranda Smith
Editorial Director: Lindsey Lowe

Consultant Editor
Peter Lewis
Writer and Editor for the American Geographical
Society, New York

Author
Robyn Hardyman

Picture Credits
Front Cover: Shutterstock: William Casey, Polartern (t),
Chlorophylle (b).

Alamy Images: Caro 26r, Dennis Hallinan 22r, The
London Art Archive 21t; Corbis: Marco Bucco/EPA 28b,
Sandro Vannini 29b; Fotolia: 16t; Getty Images: Shaun
Botterill 12-13; Istockphoto: 3c, 5l, 9t, 9b, 11tl, 13c, 18t,
24l, 27c; Science Photo Library: Royal Astronomical
Society 9r; Shutterstock: 3t, 3b, 4b, 6c, 8t, 8l, 8r, 10c, 11tr,
11b, 13r, 14t, 14b, 15l, 15r, 16b, 17, 18b, 19t, 19cl, 19bl,
20t, 20b, 21c, 21br, 23tl, 23tr, 23b, 24r, 25r, 26l, 27t, 27b,
28-29, 29r, Wikipedia: 12l

Artworks and maps © The Brown Reference Group Lt

Contents

Welcome to Italy

Italy has been a single, united nation for less than 150 years (see page 8). The landscape of Italy varies greatly, from high mountains in the north to sunny beaches in the south. The whole country, however, has a rich cultural history, which makes it one of the most popular destinations in the world for visitors.

The **peninsula** of Italy is divided into twenty regions, and each one has a capital city. For example, Milan is the capital of Lombardy and Naples is the capital of Campania. Each region also has its own local government and a **president**. The whole country is then united under a president and a **prime minister**.

France

Switzerland

Austria

Slovenia

Italy

Italy

Mediterranean Sea

Sicily

Venice
Venice is a city in northern Italy. It is built on 120 tiny islands that are connected by about 400 bridges. Instead of roads, Venice has canals of sea water. People get from place to place in long, narrow boats known as gondolas (right).

Italian borders

Italy mostly borders the Mediterranean Sea, but it has land borders with France, Switzerland, Austria and Slovenia.

ITALIAN FACTS

FULL NAME	Italian Republic
CAPITAL CITY	Rome
AREA	301,335 square km
POPULATION IN 2008	58,147,733
MAIN LANGUAGE	Italian
MAIN RELIGION	Roman Catholic
CURRENCY	Euro

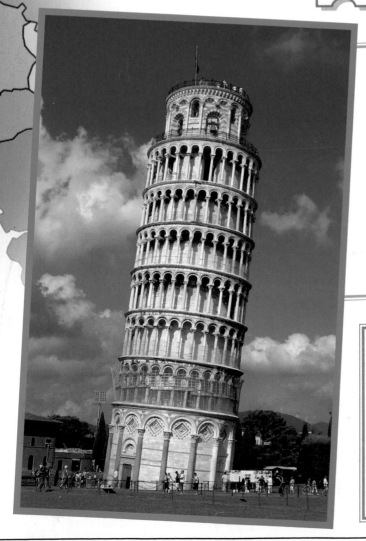

Leaning Tower of Pisa

The Leaning Tower of Pisa is the bell tower of Pisa's cathedral. It is one of the most famous buildings in the world. It began to lean soon after building began in 1173, because its foundations were laid badly. Between 1990 and 2001 the tower was partly straightened, so today it is stable.

Emblem of Italy

This is the **emblem** of Italy. It appears on the cover of an Italian European passport.

History Highlights

Two thousand years ago, Italy was at the centre of a great empire. The Roman Empire at its height, in about 170 C.E., included most of western Europe, the Middle East and North Africa.

In 410 C.E. **barbarian** tribes invaded the empire and captured Rome. In the following centuries, the buildings and other parts of ancient Roman life fell into ruin. Italy was not a single united country, but a collection of smaller states each centred on a major city. These **city-states** were ruled by powerful families. For several centuries there was fighting between the city-states.

Colosseum

The Colosseum is an amphitheatre. It was the biggest building in ancient Rome. Wild animal shows and gladiator fights were held here in front of audiences of up to 50,000 people.

WEB LINKS
To find out more about ancient Rome go to:
www.bbc.co.uk/schools/romans/index.shtml

Marco Polo

Marco Polo (1254–1324) was one of the few Europeans to visit China in the Middle Ages. In 1271 he began an extraordinary journey by camel along the **Silk Road**, a long road from China to Iran that linked China to the West. Polo met the Chinese Emperor Kublai Khan (reigned 1260–94) in 1274 and spent time in his court. Polo returned to Italy twenty-four years later, and wrote about his adventures.

The Roman army

The Roman army was the best organized and best trained army in the world. Roman soldiers were not only powerful fighters, but also skilled engineers. The Roman army built forts, roads and bridges in countries they conquered, many of which still stand today.

Great builders

The Romans were great **architects** and builders. Their magnificent public buildings included temples, law courts, amphitheatres, baths, and even stadiums for chariot races.

Italy becomes one country

In the fifteenth century, educated people in Italy rediscovered the art and science of ancient Greece and Rome in a movement called the **Renaissance** (rebirth). Conflict between the city-states continued, however, and Italy was ruled first by Spain (1559–1713) and then by Austria (1713–96). In the nineteenth century the city-states united, and in 1870 Italy became a single nation, ruled by a king, Victor Emmanuel III. The Pope would not accept **unification** (union). He continued to rule the Vatican City, which, as a **principality**, is still independent of the rest of Italy today.

Vatican City

Rome

DID YOU KNOW?
The smallest country in the world is the Vatican City. It is only 44 hectares large and is surrounded by a high wall. The city lies within Rome and has its own supermarket, post office, bank, police force, fire brigade, railway station, electricity generating plant, radio and television centre.

Protecting the Pope
The Swiss Guard have been protecting the Pope in the Vatican since 1506. Although their uniforms are decorative, they are highly trained soldiers.

Galileo Galilei

Galileo Galilei (1564–1642) was a scientist, mathematician and **astronomer**. He was one of the first people to look at space through a telescope. Galileo was convinced that the Earth and planets moved around the Sun at a time when most people thought the opposite was true.

Phases of the Moon
Galileo made these detailed drawings of the phases of the Moon, as he saw them through his telescope.

Italy and the World Wars

In World War I, Italy sided with Britain, France and the United States against Germany and Austria. After the war, however, a **dictator** called Benito Mussolini came to power in Italy. Mussolini formed an alliance with the German leader Adolf Hitler. Italy entered World War II on the side of Germany. After the war, Italians voted to become a **republic**. This stamp from World War II shows Mussolini (right) with Hitler (left).

Fly the Flag

The national flag of Italy has three vertical stripes of green, white and red. It is known as the tricolore, which means 'three colours'. The green side of the Italian flag is attached to a flagpole.

Until Italy became one united nation in 1870, each state had its own flag. Between 1848 and 1870, the tricolore was a symbol that united the Italian people in their struggle towards freedom and independence. Between 1870 and 1947, the flag had on it the coat of arms of the ruling royal family, the House of Savoy.

Giuseppe Garibaldi

Giuseppe Garibaldi (1807–82) is an Italian national hero. It was under his leadership that Italian soldiers brought many city-states under control, which helped to create a united Italy.

House of Savoy

This is the Italian flag at the time of the House of Savoy. On the state flag the shield had a crown above it.

Vatican City

This is the flag of the Vatican City. It features the crossed keys of Saint Peter and the Papal Tiara, or Pope's crown. Saint Peter was the first head of the Catholic Church and the Pope is the head today.

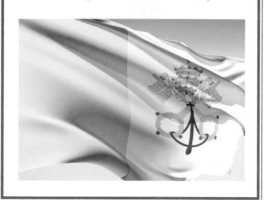

DID YOU KNOW?
The inspiration for the colours and design of the modern Italian flag came from the French flag. Some northern Italian city-states adopted the colours of the French flag during Napoleon's invasion of Italy in 1796. The red, white and green design of the national Italian flag was later based on the flags of these northern city-states.

Try this!

Make an Italian pencil holder

- *On a piece of white paper mark out three rectangles 5 cm wide by about 15 cm long. Paint one rectangle green and one red. Leave the third one white.*

- *When the paint has dried, cut out the three rectangles.*

- *Trim a cardboard tube from inside a kitchen roll so that it is 15 cm long.*

- *Cut out a circle of card a little bigger than one end of the tube, and make small cuts round its edge. Stick this over one end, folding the cut pieces up around the sides, to form the base of the pot.*

- *Now stick the coloured rectangles around the tube. Put green at the top, then white, then red. Trim them to fit exactly round the tube.*

Hymn to Italy

Italy's colourful and dramatic history has meant that the country has had more than one national anthem since unification.

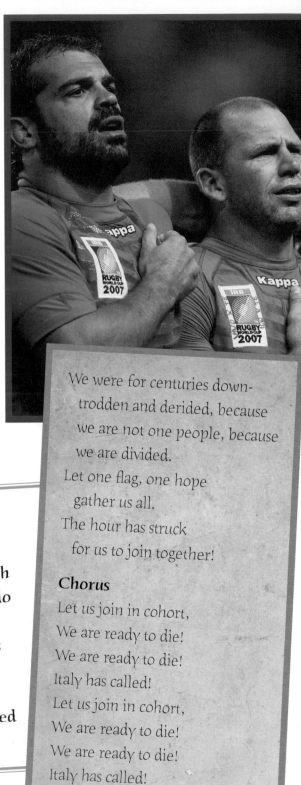

*I*l Canto degli Italiani ('The Song of the Italians') is the Italian **national anthem** today. It is best known among Italians as *Inno di Mameli* ('Mameli's Hymn'), or *Fratelli d'Italia* ('Brothers of Italy'). The words were written in 1847 by a student from Genoa named Goffredo Mameli. They refer to Italy's struggle for unification and independence.

We were for centuries down-trodden and derided, because we are not one people, because we are divided.
Let one flag, one hope gather us all.
The hour has struck for us to join together!

Chorus
Let us join in cohort,
We are ready to die!
We are ready to die!
Italy has called!
Let us join in cohort,
We are ready to die!
We are ready to die!
Italy has called!

Goffredo Mameli
On the right is one verse of the national anthem with its rousing chorus. Goffredo Mameli wrote the words when he was only 20 years old. He was injured defending the Roman Republic against the French in 1849 and died a month later at the age of 22.

Rugby song

The Italian rugby team (left), and fans of the national football team (below), proudly sing the national anthem at their international matches.

Mameli's Hymn was first written without words. Two months after he composed it, the writer Michele Novaro wrote the words.

WEB LINKS ▼▼▼▼▼▼▼▼▼▼▼▼▼
To hear the Italian national anthem go to:
www.national-anthems.net/IT

An earlier anthem

After unification in 1870, Italy chose a song called the *Marcia Reale* (below) as its anthem. This remained the national anthem until Italy became a republic in 1947. Then *The Song of the Italians* was chosen as the new anthem. This choice was only formally accepted in 2005, almost sixty years later.

Regions of Italy

Italy forms a peninsula that faces southeast into the Mediterranean Sea. The islands of Sicily, Sardinia, Elba and Capri are also part of the country. So too are the separate principalities of Vatican City and San Marino.

I taly has dramatic mountains, grassy plains and beautiful beaches. In the north, winters are cold and summers are hot. The best agricultural (farming) land is in the north. Most industry is there also. The south is warmer, with a **Mediterranean climate**. Here the land is not as fertile, and there is less industry.

A land of mountains

Italy has three mountain ranges: the Alps in the northwest, the Dolomites in the northeast and the Apennines, which extend for 1,360 kilometres down the centre of the country.

Wildlife
The rare ibex lives in the Gran Paradiso national park in northwest Italy.

Coastal beauty

The Amalfi Coast is a stretch of coastline on the west coast of Italy. Famous for its rugged terrain, scenic beauty and picturesque towns, the Amalfi Coast is a World Heritage Site.

ITALIAN FACTS

LONGEST RIVERS	Po 652 km, Adige 410 km
HIGHEST MOUNTAIN	Great Horn in the Apennines 2,912 m
LARGEST CITIES	Rome, Milan, Naples, Turin
NATIONAL PARKS	Twenty-one national parks

Sicily

The beautiful island of Sicily in the Mediterranean Sea is part of Italy. Sicily has been occupied by many peoples over the centuries, so it has many historic sites. At Syracuse, an ancient Greek theatre (below) stands to this day. Plays are still performed there.

Volcanoes

Sicily's Mount Etna is one of the world's most active volcanoes. Its lava flows destroy local villages every few years. Mount Vesuvius, near Naples, erupts less often, but can be devastating. Its eruption of 79 C.E. buried the towns of Pompeii (above) and Herculaneum.

What's Cooking?

Italian pasta and pizza are popular throughout the world. Both of these are typical Italian dishes, but each region of Italy has its own specialities.

I n central Italy, olive oil and beef are specialities of Tuscany, while Parmesan cheese and Parma ham are made in Emilia–Romagna in the north. The south has superb fruit, herbs and seafood, and many dishes use tomatoes. Many of Italy's finest cheeses are made in the north.

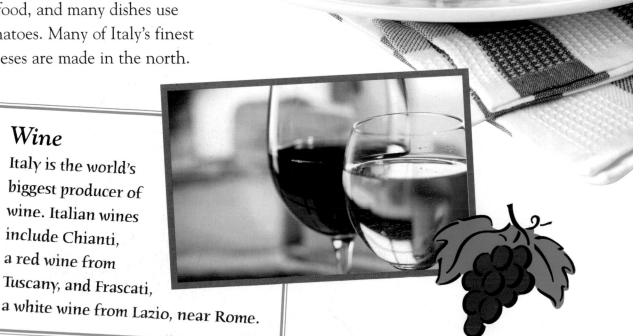

Wine

Italy is the world's biggest producer of wine. Italian wines include Chianti, a red wine from Tuscany, and Frascati, a white wine from Lazio, near Rome.

DID YOU KNOW?

The Italians serve their coffee in many different ways. A cappuccino is coffee mixed with hot milk and topped with foamy milk. A caffelatte is strong coffee mixed with hot milk. An espresso is a very small and strong coffee, which is served in a tiny cup.

Spaghetti sauce

The Bolognese sauce on this spaghetti was first created in the city of Bologna.

What's on the menu?

A full Italian meal has the following courses:

antipasto (starter)
sliced salami

il primo (first course)
tagliatelle (ribbon pasta) with butter and sage

il secondo (main course)
vitello (veal) with lemon sauce and green beans

dolce (dessert)
tiramisu (creamy pudding) or gelati (ice cream) formaggio (cheese) espresso (strong, small coffee)

Try this!

Let's make fusilli al tonno (tuna pasta)

Ingredients:
400 g fusilli (spiral pasta)
50 ml olive oil
1 small onion, chopped
1 clove of garlic, crushed
125 g tinned tuna
400 g tin chopped tomatoes
salt and pepper

Put the olive oil, crushed garlic and chopped onion in a frying pan. Fry over a low heat until the onion is golden brown. Add the chopped tomatoes, salt and pepper. Cook gently for about 5 minutes, and then add the tuna. Cook gently for a further 10 minutes. While the sauce is cooking, bring a saucepan full of water to the boil. When it is bubbling, ask an adult to add the fusilli pasta. Boil for 10 minutes. Ask an adult to drain the pasta and return it to the saucepan. Add the sauce to the pasta and stir well. Serve on to warmed plates.

How Do I Say...?

For most people in Italy their first language is the dialect of their local region. Most people also speak Italian.

Modern Italian comes from Latin, the language of the ancient Romans, and then from the **dialect** of Tuscany, a region in northern Italy. The Tuscan dialect became the most widely used because the three great writers of the Middle Ages – Dante, Boccaccio, and Petrarch – wrote in the Tuscan dialect.

Words and phrases

English	Italian	How to say it
hello	buon giorno	bwon jaw-no
goodbye	arrivederci	aree-ved-air-chee
please	per favore	pair fav-oray
thank you	grazie	grat-zee-ay
yes	si	see
no	no	noh
Excuse me	Mi scusi	me skoo-zee
How are you?	Come sta?	kom-ay stah
My name is ...	Mi chiama ...	me kee-ama

Some slang expressions

È di luna buona ('There is a beautiful moon'). 'He/she is in a good mood.'

Parlare fuori dai denti. 'To speak outside of one's teeth.' This means to say what is on your mind.

Modern Italian

Ancient Romans spoke a language called Latin. The words carved into this ancient stone tablet are in Latin. Modern Italian has grown out of the Latin language and many Italian words are very similar to Latin ones.

Italian sayings

Ho una fame da lupi.
'I'm as hungry as a wolf.'

Chi trova un amico trova un tesoro.
'Who finds a friend finds a treasure.'

DID YOU KNOW?
The informal word *ciao* can be used to mean either 'hello' or 'goodbye'.

WEB LINKS
To hear more contemporary Italian expressions go to:
www.italianlanguageguide.com/italian/grammar/exclamation.asp

Stories and Legends

There are hundreds of folk tales in Italian literature. They take readers into a world of adventurers, tricksters, kings, maidens, peasants and saints. The children's stories of Cinderella and Pinocchio were originally Italian folk tales.

In one Italian story, Parrot, a handsome prince, must save the woman he loves from being taken away by an evil king. The prince turns himself into a parrot and holds the woman's attention by telling her an enchanting tale until she is safe from danger.

Romulus and Remus

According to legend, the city of Rome was founded in 753 B.C.E. by Romulus and Remus. These twin boys were the sons of the god Mars. They were abandoned, but found and raised by a wolf. The city's name comes from Romulus.

DID YOU KNOW?
In Rome, in a wall of the church called Santa Maria in Cosmedin, there is an ancient marble sculpture called *La Bocca della Verità* ('the mouth of truth'). In the Middle Ages people used this statue as a lie detector by speaking with their hand inside the mouth of the sculpture. They believed that if they told a lie, the sculpture would bite off their hand!

Dante Alighieri

Dante Alighieri (1265–1321) is Italy's most famous poet. His greatest work was *The Divine Comedy*, a very long poem that tells of his travels through the three realms of the dead: Hell, Purgatory and Paradise. Dante is sometimes called 'the Father of the Italian language'.

Pinocchio

This famous story is about a wooden boy puppet that comes to life. It was written by an Italian, Carlo Collodi, and published in 1883. Pinocchio's nose grows longer every time he tells a lie and he learns about life through his adventures.

Tarantula dance

In medieval legend, the women of the town of Taranto were bitten by tarantulas (spiders). The bites sent the women into a trance, from which they could only be cured by frenzied dancing! The *tarantella* dance is today performed by Italians on special occasions.

WEB LINKS
Find out more about the story of Romulus and Remus at:
www.historyonthenet.com/Romans/legend_of_rome.htm

Art and Culture

Italy has a magnificent cultural history. The Italian Renaissance produced some of the greatest artists ever seen. Since then, painters, architects, musicians and artists of many kinds have lived and worked in the country.

Leonardo da Vinci (1452–1519) and Michelangelo Buonarroti (1475–1564) were two of the greatest artists of the Italian Renaissance. They both trained in Florence, and were great rivals. Michelangelo painted with a realistic style and power that had not been seen before. Leonardo was interested in revealing people's personalities in his paintings. He was a brilliant inventor and scientist as well.

Siena Town Hall
The magnificent town hall in Siena is part of one of the finest medieval squares in Italy.

Oldest festival
Florence's 'Maggio Musicale' is one of Italy's oldest music festivals. It features opera, orchestras and ballet.

Films

The Cinecittà Studios in Rome are the largest in Europe. Many classic films were made there in the 1950s and 1960s, including *Ben Hur* (1959). Zeffirelli's *Romeo and Juliet* was also made there in 1968.

A mysterious smile

The Mona Lisa, by Leonardo da Vinci, is one of the most famous paintings in the world. It is a portrait of Lisa del Giocondo, the wife of a wealthy sixteenth-century Italian merchant. The painting of Lisa, with her mysterious smile, has become one of the most talked about works of art in history.

Opera

Opera is a combination of classical music, singing and drama. It began in Italy in the sixteenth century. Famous Italian operas include *Rigoletto* by Verdi and *Tosca* by Puccini.

Statue of David

Michelangelo's Statue of David is the most famous stone sculpture in the history of art. It portrays the Biblical King David as a youth about to battle with the giant Goliath. The statue is 5.2 m high.

Fashion

Italians love to look smart and fashionable. Italian fashion designers such as Armani, Gucci, Prada and Versace are famous all over the world. The northern city of Milan is one of the fashion capitals of the world.

Make Your Own Pizza Solitaire

Try making this solitaire board that looks like a pizza with olives! You play by jumping any counter over its neighbour so that you can remove that counter. The aim is to end up with just one counter left, in the centre of the board. Remember – the pizza is a game and is not meant to be eaten!

1 Preheat the oven to 120°C/gas mark ½. Mix the flour, salt, oil and water in a bowl.

2 Knead the mixture with your hands until it is no longer sticky. Sprinkle a surface with flour and use a rolling pin to roll out the dough. Use a large plate to mark a circle in the dough and cut it out.

3 Line a baking tray with foil and lay the dough inside. Cut out a circle of white paper the same size as the pizza. Draw a circle 1 cm in from the edge of the paper, and a pattern of dots.

4 Lay the paper over the pizza and use the toothpick to prick through the dots and along the circle. Cut a few tomato, mushroom and fish shapes from the leftover dough and press them on the pizza.

DID YOU KNOW?
Italians eat many different things. A few of the unusual items you might be served in an Italian restaurant are snails, horse, donkey, goat, wild boar, peacock, hedgehogs, guinea pigs, sea urchins, sea snails, octopus and squid!

Ancient pizza

A preserved flat flour cake was found in the volcanic ashes of Pompeii, the town destroyed by Vesuvius in 79 C.E. The cake is typical of the food eaten in Pompeii in Roman times, and is believed to be the world's oldest pizza.

5 Remove the paper and use the saucer to make a groove along the inner circle. Press a small marble into the toothpick holes to make dents.

6 Roll 32 marble-sized counters out of the dough, so they fit in the dents on the pizza. Put them on a separate lined baking tray. Ask an adult to bake the board and counters in the oven for 30 minutes. Allow them to cool.

7 Roll the counters in a saucer of watery black paint so they look like olives. Paint the pizza, tomatoes, mushrooms and fish using poster paints. Add a layer of varnish when the paints are dry.

Sports and Leisure

Italians work hard, but they also enjoy their free time. They like to relax with family and friends over a meal, to travel and to play sports. Football, rugby, cycling, swimming and skiing are all popular sports in Italy.

Football is Italy's favourite sport. Most cities have their own teams, which play in tournaments. Their national football team is one of the best in the world. It has won the World Cup four times: in 1934, 1938, 1982 and 2006. Many Italians like to play football, too.

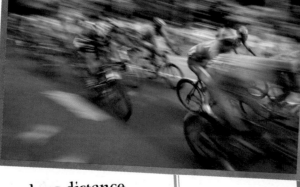

Giro d'Italia

The Giro d'Italia is a world-famous long-distance bicycle race, held in Italy in May. The route of the 2008 race was more than 3,360 km long.

WEB LINKS ▼▼▼▼▼▼▼▼▼▼

The official website of the Giro d'Italia is:
www.gazzetta.it/Speciali/Giroditalia/2008/en/

Water sports

Italy has a lot of coastline. The windswept coast of Sardinia is popular for fishing and water sports.

Corsica

Mainland Italy

Sardinia

Fabio Cannavaro

The Italian Fabio Cannavaro (born in Naples in 1973) is a World Cup-winning footballer. He was made captain of Italy's national football team in 2002. At club level he plays for Real Madrid. Cannavaro was voted Fifa World Player of the Year in 2006.

Family

For many Italians their family is the most important part of their lives. Traditionally, several generations of a family live very near to each other, sometimes in the same house. This is becoming less common today, but Italians still like to spend their free time with family members. It is often an occasion for a large meal and a party.

San Siro

San Siro is the home stadium for two of Milan's football teams: A.C. Milan and F.C. Internazionale. It is considered to have one of the best atmospheres of any stadium in the world.

Festivals and Holidays

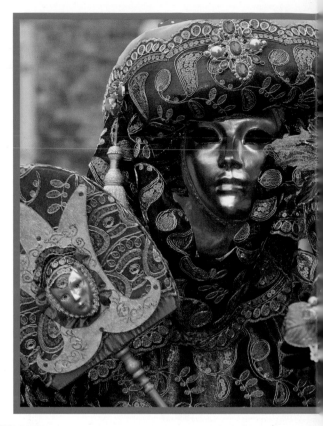

There are thousands of festivals in Italy each year. These can be important national or religious festivals, or small local celebrations.

Most Italians are Roman Catholic. As well as the major religious holidays, such as Christmas and Easter, Italian cities celebrate a local feast day for their patron saint. The festival for Rome's patron saint is on 29th June, and Milan's is on 7th December.

The Palio

Every summer the city of Siena holds the Palio, an exciting horse race that takes place in July and then again in August. The race dates back to 1310. In a thrilling competition, bareback riders, representing each district of the city, race at top speed three times around the main square. A banner, called the Palio, is presented to the winner. It is decorated with an image of the Virgin Mary.

DID YOU KNOW?
The Palio is over in 90 seconds, but a parade, and a display of flag-waving and flag-throwing takes place before it.

Carnival

Carnevale (meaning 'carnival') is held each year in February. People wear bright costumes and enjoy parades and masked balls. The tradition dates from the fourteenth century. Venice is especially famous for its carnival masks.

Food and wine festivals

Rural areas hold local festivals all year round. These are often linked to a particular seasonal food, such as mushrooms or olive oil, or are a celebration of the wine harvest. The people of the village gather for dinner at long tables in the street. After eating, they listen to music and dance.

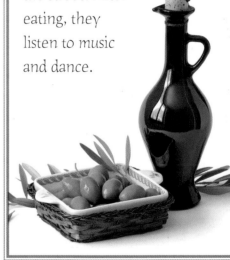

Republic Day

2nd June is Republic Day in Italy. This public holiday commemorates the day when Italy became a republic.

Calabrian festival

Every September, Italians travel to a holy site in Calabria, Italy, called the Sanctuary of Saint Maria de Polsi. A festival takes place in celebration of the many miracles believed to have occurred there.

Glossary

ampitheatre oval or circular building with tiers of seats around an arena

architects people who design buildings

astronomer person who studies the stars, planets and space

barbarian person considered to be uneducated and primitive

city-states independent regions much like a country but smaller, consisting of a city and the surrounding territory

climate the average weather conditions over a long period of time

dialect language spoken by people in one region of a country

dictator person who rules a country in a harsh, overbearing way, not allowing anyone to disagree with them

emblem symbol that represents a country

foundations lowest part of a building that helps to support that building

gladiator in ancient Rome, a prisoner, criminal or slave trained to fight to the death against animals or another gladiator in a public show

gondolas long, narrow boats that are pushed along with a long pole; gondolas are used to travel along the canals of Venice

medieval describes the Middle Ages; this period of history was from about 400 to 1450

Mediterranean part of an area of Europe that is found around the Mediterranean Sea, includes countries such as Italy, France, Greece and Spain

national anthem official song of a country

opera play in which the words are sung to music instead of spoken

peninsula piece of land that is surrounded by water on three sides

president person who runs a country, voted for by its people

prime minister person elected by the people to run a country

principality country ruled by a prince

Renaissance rebirth; a revival of the art and ideas of ancient Greece and Rome that began in Italy in the late fourteenth century

republic a state in which the head of government is not a monarch; republics usually have elected presidents

Silk Road route along which merchants from China took silk to Europe

unification union; joining together of two states

Find Out More

Books

Anderson, Maxine. *Amazing Leonardo Da Vinci Inventions You Can Build Yourself*
Nomad
ISBN: 978 0 9749 3442 6

Borlenghi, Patricia. *Find Out About: Italy*
Franklin Watts
ISBN: 978 0 7496 7732 9

Clements, Gillian. *A Picture History of Great Buildings*. Frances Lincoln
ISBN: 978 1 8450 7488 3

Pirotta, Saviour. *Italy Festivals and Food*
Wayland
ISBN 978 0 7502 4843 3

Thomson, Ruth. *Living in: Italy*
Franklin Watts
ISBN: 978 0 7496 6340 7

Wright, Rachel. *Country Topics Italy*
Franklin Watts
ISBN: 978 0 7496 7335 2

Websites

http://kids.yahoo.com/reference/world-factbook/country/it--italy
An excellent website that contains many facts about Italy and its people.

www.italianfoodforever.com
You will find lots of delicious recipes for Italian food here.

www.italiantourism.com
You can explore Italy by region at the official site of the Italian tourist board.

www.italyguides.it/us/roma/rome_italy_travel.htm
This site has virtual tours of twelve cities in Italy, including Rome, Venice, Naples, Siena, Florence and Palermo.

www.pocanticohills.org/italy/italy.htm
Read about Italian life, look at pictures and play games at this site created by a school in New York.

www.vatican.va
Meet the Pope at official website of the world's smallest country, Vatican City.

Index